Tikky Tikky SPIDER

By Joy Cowley

Illustrated by Jenny Press

⌐ Dominie Press, Inc.

Publisher: Christine Yuen
Editor: John S. F. Graham
Designer: Lois Stanfield
Illustrator: Jenny Press

Published by:

🔶 **Dominie Press, Inc.**

1949 Kellogg Avenue
Carlsbad, California 92008 USA

www.dominie.com

Paperback ISBN 0-7685-1079-1
Library Bound Edition ISBN 0-7685-1526-2
Printed in Singapore by PH Productions Pte Ltd
  2 3 4 5 6 PH 04 03

Table of Contents

Chapter One

Storm Cloud and Lightning

Once upon a time,
when the world was still new,
there lived a brother and a sister
who could dance like the wind.

Oh yes! Oh Yes!

His name was Storm Cloud,
and her name was Lightning,
and when people saw them dancing,
they shook their rattles
and beat their drums
and sang songs that made
the flowers open.

Oh yes!

Now, Storm Cloud and Lightning
lived in a very fine place.
There was only one thing wrong.

In the forest nearby,
lived Tikky Tikky Spider.

Tikky Tikky was the biggest spider
that had ever lived on Earth.
Its body was as big as a buffalo,
and it had legs
like the branches of a tree.
Its eyes were as big as red melons.
It had a mean, sharp mouth
that could eat a whole cow
for lunch.

Goocha-goocha-gulp!

Oh yes!

This was a nighttime spider
that could not stand the sun.
So during the day,
the cattle were safe.

But at night, Tikky Tikky Spider
came out of the forest
to spin a sticky silk web
around a cow.

Oh no! Oh no!

Oh yes!

In the morning, all that was left
were a few white bones
in the sticky ropes of the web.

Chapter Two
Around and Around

Storm Cloud and Lightning
had three cows: one red,
one brown, and one black-and-white.
During the day,
the cows fed on grass,
but at night
Storm Cloud and Lightning put them
in the house to keep them safe.

When the stars were out,
Tikky Tikky Spider
could smell those nice, fat cows
in the house.

Oh yes!

That spider walked
around and around,
like the shadow of a mountain,
looking for a way in.

One night,
Storm Cloud and Lightning
were dancing at a wedding party.

So loud was the drumming
and singing,
they did not hear
the bellowing of the cows.

Goocha-goocha-gulp!
Oh no! Oh no!

When they went back home,
they found the door pushed open.
The black-and-white cow was gone!

Oh yes!

Chapter Three
A Hole in the Roof

After that,
Storm Cloud and Lightning
stayed with their cows each night.

But then a baby was born
in the village,
and they were asked to dance
to celebrate the new life.

They put bars of wood
across their door
to keep out Tikky Tikky Spider.
Then they went to the party.

So loud was the drumming,
so loud was the laughter,
that no one heard
the bellowing of the cows.

Goocha-goocha-gulp!

Oh no! Oh no!

When the children returned home,
they saw a hole
in the roof of their house.
The brown cow was gone.

Oh yes!

Chapter Four

Are You Hungry, Tikky Tikky?

The children had only
the red cow left,
and a fine, sweet cow it was, too.
They looked after that cow
with great care.

They mended the roof
and made it strong,
and every night they kept watch
for that greedy Tikky Tikky Spider.

They knew it would be back.

Oh yes!

As sure as fire is hot,
as sure as water is wet,
Tikky Tikky Spider came looking
for that sweet, red cow.

Like the shadow of a mountain
it came, sneaking around the house,
its eyes like big, red melons,
its mouth all sharp with teeth,
remembering the taste of cow.

But this time,
Storm Cloud and Lightning
had a clever plan.

Oh yes! Oh yes!

When they heard the spider,
Storm Cloud ran out
into the darkness and danced
in front of those big, red eyes
and that mean, sharp mouth.

"Are you hungry, Tikky Tikky?"
Storm Cloud shouted.
"Then try me!
I am young, and I am sweet.
I am better than cow to eat."

The big spider turned
and ran after him,
its eight legs
swishing through the grass.
But Storm Cloud danced and danced,
and the spider could not catch him.

When Storm Cloud became tired,
it was Lightning's turn.

She jumped out
in front of the Spider.
"What about me, Tikky Tikky?"

Lightning danced and danced,
with the spider running after her.

Chapter Five

An Old
Spider Trick

Tikky Tikky was very hungry.
When it saw that the children
were too fast for it,
it tried an old spider trick.
It ran around them,
spinning a sticky thread
as thick as a rope.

Around and around it went,
until it had spun a thick web
that encircled them.

If they touched the strands,
they would be stuck,
and Tikky Tikky would eat them.

"What will we do, brother?"
cried Lightning.
"Keep dancing!" said Storm Cloud.
"It is nearly morning."

24

Although they were tired,
the children kept on dancing.
And the spider kept on spinning.

The web was getting closer, closer.

Storm Cloud and Lightning
noticed that the sky was gray.

"Keep dancing!" said Storm Cloud.
But the web was now so close
that there was nowhere to go.

Another moment,
and Tikky Tikky Spider
would have them.

Oh no! Oh no!

They saw the red eyes above them.
They saw the pointed teeth.
Tikky Tikky Spider
was going to eat them!

Oh no! Oh no!

Then the sun came up
over the forest
like a big, orange ball,
and the earth was filled with light.

Oh yes! Oh yes!

Then a strange thing
happened to the spider.

It squealed and began to shrink.
It tried to hide from the sun.

It hunched up its legs
and lowered its head,
but the sun shone down on it,
and the spider kept on getting
smaller and smaller.

Its web, too, became small,
so small that it got lost in the grass.

Storm Cloud and Lightning watched
as the shrinking spider
ran toward their house.

It could do no harm now.
It ran up the door
like the shadow of a peanut
and hid in the thatch of the roof.

It would never eat cow again.

To this day,
the children of Tikky Tikky Spider
live in people's houses.

Sometimes they tell stories
about the taste of cow,
but they are so small,
all they can catch are flies.

Oh yes! Oh yes!